AN ASSESSMENT OF THE DEPARTMENT OF DEFENSE STRATEGY FOR OPERATING IN CYBERSPACE

INTRODUCTION

Computer networks have become essential to the proper operation of the U.S. Government and military. According to then Secretary of Defense Robert Gates, the Department of Defense (DoD) operates "more than 15,000 local, regional, and wide-area networks, and approximately seven million information technology (IT) devices."[1] The increasing reliance on computer networks has created opportunities for foreign nations, terrorists, "hacktivists," and criminals. Government networks are being constantly probed for vulnerabilities and have occasionally been compromised, resulting in the theft of considerable amounts of sensitive data. Several intrusions have been publicly disclosed, including:

- Moonlight Maze involved 2 years of infiltrations starting in 1998 into the Pentagon, National Aeronautics and Space Administration (NASA), Department of Energy (DoE), and affiliated labs. Tens of thousands of files, including military maps, U.S. troop configurations, military hardware designs, and naval codes were reportedly compromised. According to congressional testimony of James Adams, chief executive officer of Infrastructure Defense, Inc., the stolen information was "shipped over the Internet to Moscow for sale to the highest bidder."[2]
- Titan Rain was a series of intrusions starting in 2003 into computer systems at Sandia National

Labs, NASA, Redstone Arsenal military base, World Bank, and various defense contractors. Military intelligence was stolen, including Army helicopter specifications, Falconview (flight planning software), and aerospace documents.[3]

- Intrusions into defense contractor information systems in 2007 and 2008 reportedly allowed an unidentified foreign country to exfiltrate successfully "several terabytes of data related to design and electronics systems" of the F-35 *Lightning II*, an advanced fighter plane.[4]
- In March 2011, Deputy Defense Secretary William Lynn admitted that "terabytes of data have been extracted by foreign intruders from corporate networks of (unnamed) defense companies."[5] The theft involved 24,000 files of data ranging from specifications for small parts on tanks, airplanes, and submarines to aircraft avionics, surveillance technologies, satellite communications systems, and network security protocols.

As cyberspace has become increasingly important, the U.S. Government has issued a number of publications on national cybersecurity strategy leading up to the 2011 *DoD Strategy for Operating in Cyberspace*. Some themes have been repeated often, such as a need for public-private sector cooperation, reduction of vulnerabilities, more cyber security training, and international cooperation. A summary of these documents is listed in the appendix.

An Evolution of Cyberspace Strategies.

In February 2003, President George Bush issued the *National Strategy to Secure Cyberspace*.[6] It highlighted three strategic priorities:

1. Prevent cyber attacks against America's critical infrastructure;

2. Reduce national vulnerability to cyber attacks; and,

3. Minimize damage and recovery time from cyber attacks, and identified five critical national priorities:

    a. Implement a national cyberspace security response system;

    b. Reduce cyberspace threats and vulnerabilities;

    c. Increase national cyber security awareness and training;

    d. Secure government cyberspace;

    e. Enhance national and international cyberspace cooperation.

The primary aim of the strategy was to improve cyber security nationwide, not only government systems but also critical infrastructures owned by the private sector. For each of the five national priorities, several major "actions and initiatives" were spelled out. Among these, several are noteworthy:

- Encourage public-private partnerships for cyber incident response;
- Improve public-private information sharing involving cyber attacks, threats, and vulnerabilities;
- Prioritize federal research and development (R&D) in cyber security;
- Foster training and education programs in cyber security;

- Strengthen cyber-related counterintelligence efforts;
- Improve capabilities for attack attribution and response;
- Establish international partnerships to protect information infrastructures;
- Establish national and international watch-and-warning networks to detect and prevent cyber attacks.

Most of the themes reappear in the 2011 *DoD Strategy for Operating in Cyberspace* (e.g., national and international cooperation, public-private partnerships and information sharing, reduction of vulnerabilities, and cyber security awareness).

In 2004, the Joint Chiefs of Staff published the *National Military Strategy of the United States of America*.[7] It was an action plan for the Armed Forces to support the *National Security Strategy* and *National Defense Strategy*. It emphasized three priorities: fighting terrorism; enhancing joint warfighting; and transforming the joint force to meet military objectives in the near and far terms. It notably included cyberspace as one of the domains of the battlespace along with air, land, sea, and space.

Two years later, the Joint Chiefs of Staff published the *National Military Strategy for Cyberspace Operations* (NMS-CO) focused specifically on cyber security.[8] It aimed to characterize the cyberspace domain, identify threats and vulnerabilities, and propose a strategic framework to assure U.S. military superiority in cyberspace. The NMS-CO appeared to significantly influence the 2011 *DoD Strategy for Operating in Cyberspace,* where the main themes reappeared.

The NMS-CO identified six enabling ways to maintain superiority in cyberspace, including these three:

1. Investment in science and technology;
2. Partnerships with industry, government agencies, and other nations; and,
3. Investment in a trained workforce.

It also named four strategic priorities:

1. Gain and maintain initiative to operate within adversarial decision cycles;
2. Integrate cyberspace capabilities across the range of military operations;
3. Build capacity for cyberspace operations; and,
4. Manage risk for operations in cyberspace.

Each strategic priority was accompanied by several specific initiatives.

In August 2007, President Bush established the Commission on Cybersecurity for the 44th Presidency to examine the national cyber security strategy for areas for improvement. At its conclusion, the commission stated that cyberspace was an urgent national security problem and recommended 25 actions.[9]

In the meantime, President Bush enacted the Comprehensive National Cybersecurity Initiative (CNCI) aimed at improving the capabilities of the Department of Homeland Security (DHS) and other government agencies to protect against existing and future intrusions.[10] The CNCI was a number of interrelated initiatives with three major goals aimed at improving cyber security:

1. To establish a "front line of defense" against existing threats through shared situational awareness and prevent future intrusions by reducing vulnerabilities;

2. To defend against the full spectrum of threats through better counterintelligence and better security of the supply chain for key information technologies;

3. To expand cyber education; coordinate R&D across the federal government; and develop strategies to deter malicious activities.

In the CNCI, some common themes from earlier publications reappear: reduction of vulnerabilities, coordination among government agencies, public-private partnering, security of the supply chain, workforce training, and focused R&D. These themes will be repeated in the later *DoD Strategy for Operating in Cyberspace*, but a couple of concepts in the CNCI, namely deterrence and counterintelligence, were not repeated explicitly. Instead, the *DoD Strategy* addresses deterrence and counterintelligence more subtly. It hints at counterintelligence in describing the establishment of U.S. Cyber Command (USCYBERCOM), co-located with the National Security Agency (NSA) under the same director. The notion of deterrence is also addressed subtly in the description of collective security created by international cooperation; presumably, the strength of numbers will help deter future attacks.

In May 2009, President Barack Obama announced the results of a broad review of the national cyber security strategy, including CNCI. The review recommended that a new cyber security coordinator update the national strategy. The U.S. Government Accountability Office (GAO) also noted, among other recommendations, the need for a national strategy that clearly articulated strategic objectives, goals, and priorities.[11] In the same year, DHS updated its *National Infrastructure Protection Plan*, which is a framework for addressing threats to critical infrastructures relying on public-private partnerships.[12]

In May 2011, the White House released the *International Strategy for Cyberspace,* aiming to promote a global cyberspace environment that is "open, interoperable, secure, and reliable" based on "norms of responsible behavior."[13] The document is divided into three approaches for the future—diplomacy, defense, and development—and is supported by seven policy priorities. The strategy emphasized the need for international cooperation and public-private partnerships, noting that "no single institution, document, arrangement, or instrument could suffice in addressing the needs of our networked world."[14]

Whereas the *International Strategy for Cyberspace* is diplomatic, highlighting the international and cooperative aspects of a secure cyberspace, the *DoD Strategy for Operating in Cyberspace* may be considered a complementary strategy in some ways. While international cooperation is an important part of the strategy, the strategy is primarily interested in actions to ensure military superiority and protection of American assets.

DoD Strategy for Operating in Cyberspace.

In July 2011, Deputy Secretary of Defense Lynn announced the publication of a 13-page unclassified *DoD Strategy for Operating in Cyberspace* (the contents of a longer classified version has not been published).[15] The official document was preceded by a September 2010 article by Secretary Lynn. The conclusion in the article is an accurate summary of the *DoD Strategy*:

> These risks [in cyberspace] are what is driving the Pentagon to forge a new strategy for cybersecurity.

The principal elements of that strategy are to develop an organizational construct for training, equipping, and commanding cyberdefense forces; to employ layered protections with a strong core of active defenses; to use military capabilities to support other departments' efforts to secure the networks that run the United States' critical infrastructure; to build collective defenses with U.S. allies; and to invest in the rapid development of additional cyberdefense capabilities. The goal of this strategy is to make cyberspace safe so that its revolutionary innovations can enhance both the United States' national security and its economic security.[16]

The *DoD Strategy for Operating in Cyberspace* outlines five strategic initiatives to address cyber security, which can be summarized as follows:

1. Treat cyberspace as an operational domain (equivalent to air, land, maritime, and space);

2. Employ new defense operating concepts to protect DoD networks;

3. Partner with other U.S. Government agencies and the private sector;

4. Build relationships with international partners to strengthen collective security; and,

5. Invest in cyber workforce training and R&D for rapid technological innovation.

The accompanying news release described the strategy as "a new way forward for DoD's military, intelligence, and business operations."[17] Clearly, the *DoD Strategy* is significant as an official recognition of the strategic importance of cyberspace to national security. However, while the strategy is consistent with Secretary Lynn's article, the document is brief and unspecific. It repeats several themes from earlier government publications but surprisingly omits a few important ones. In the remainder of this article, each strategic initiative in the *DoD Strategy* will be examined in depth for clarity, comprehensiveness, and novelty. The implications and practicality of each initiative will be discussed. In the final section, some critical observations of the *DoD Strategy* will be made.

STRATEGIC INITIATIVE 1: DoD will treat cyberspace as an operational domain to organize, train, and equip so that DoD can take full advantage of cyberspace's potential.

This strategy initiative is an official declaration that cyberspace will be treated as the fifth operational domain in addition to air, land, sea, and space. Essentially, DoD recognizes that military operations need to extend into man-made cyberspace because cyberspace has become integral to military operations in the other domains. In modern warfare, all domains are interconnected via cyberspace operations, and cyber attacks are expected to become a common part of future conflicts. It naturally follows that DoD should build up capabilities to carry out actions in cyberspace. The strategy states "DoD will organize, train, and equip for the complex challenges and vast opportunities of cyberspace."[18]

Substantial changes have been made in organization. DoD has established the USCYBERCOM as a sub-unified command of U.S. Strategic Command (USSTRATCOM) under the Secretary of Defense. USCYBERCOM is responsible for coordinating the relevant military branches, including U.S. Army Cyber Command, U.S. Fleet Cyber Command/U.S. 10th Fleet, the 24th Air Force, U.S. Marine Corps Forces Cyber Command, and U.S. Coast Guard Cyber Command. It is deliberately co-located with the NSA under the same director. This organization is intended to maximize resources and efficiency, and directly link cyber operations with intelligence.

The *DoD Strategy* expresses concern that degraded cyberspace operations may interfere with the success of missions. To learn to operate in a possibly hostile cyberspace environment, cyber red teams will conduct war games, e.g., Cyber Storm.[19] In addition, defensive capabilities will be strengthened by investment in more resilient and secure computer networks.

Significance and Novelty.

In summary, this strategy initiative makes three points: DoD must be able to operate equally in cyberspace as in other domains; missions must succeed despite adversity in cyberspace; and cyberspace must be strengthened against threats. This initiative is a message to other government agencies, as well as to foreign countries, about the seriousness of cyber operations (and possibly military responses to cyber attacks).

As a formal statement that cyberspace will be an integral part of future warfare, this is not surprising. It recognizes the reality that most people have already accepted. The importance of military operations in cyberspace has become increasingly clear in recent years. In 2004, the Joint Chiefs of Staff issued the *National Military Strategy of the United States of America.*[20] It implied cyberspace was an operational domain by saying the military "must have the ability to operate across the air, land, sea, space, and cyberspace domains of the battlespace." In November 2006,

Secretary of the Air Force Michael W. Wynne delivered an address describing cyberspace as a warfighting domain equal to air and space: "(defend) the United States of America and its global interests—to fly and fight in air, space and cyberspace."[21] In this view, cyberspace superiority is simply an extension of air and space supremacy.

Since cyber operations are widely expected to become a critical part of military conflicts, it is logical for DoD to strive for freedom to act in cyberspace beyond civilian limitations. However, this "militarization of cyberspace" raises a few issues that are not addressed specifically in the *DoD Strategy*. First, what are the boundaries of cyberspace considered to be within military jurisdiction? Most critical network infrastructures are owned and operated by the private sector. Second, how will cyber attacks warranting a military response differentiate from other malicious acts such as cybercrime? For instance, spear phishing (social engineering) to install malware may be a tactic used in both cybercrime and military cyber espionage. Third, could cyber attacks escalate unnecessarily into physical warfare? It seems possible that DoD might classify a major cyber attack against critical infrastructure as an act of war that could trigger a conventional military response. A Pentagon official stated, "If you shut down our power grid, maybe we will put a missile down one of your smokestacks."[22] Clearly, rules need to be developed to guide appropriate responses to cyber attacks. So far, the United States has chosen not to impose any self-restrictions. Deputy Defense Secretary Lynn stated:

The United States reserves the right, under the laws of armed conflict, to respond to serious cyber attacks with a proportional and justified military response at the time and place of its choosing.[23]

Practicality.

In terms of organization, the GAO has found that progress has been made, notably the establishment of the USCYBERCOM and supporting organizations in June 2009, but more work is needed.[24] It observed that the DoD's organization to address cyber security is vast and decentralized, with responsibilities spread across various offices. The recent organizational changes are believed to be steps in the right direction, since the command will theoretically provide a "single point of accountability" but "it is too early to tell if these ongoing organizational changes will improve DoD's overall cyber efforts" to counter threats.[25]

The GAO also observed a lack of clarity about the role of civilians in conducting cyber war operations and the "mission requirements and capabilities to organize, train, and equip a cyber force."[26] Another concern was a lack of direction from USCYBERCOM about the command and control relationships between the command and regional military commanders.

In terms of investment in more resilient and secure computer networks, the *DoD Strategy* is not specific about how investment will be carried out. Researchers in resilient networks have investigated advanced technologies such as self-healing and intrusion tolerance for many years. Resilience was one of the original main design goals for the Internet.[27] Self-healing is a more advanced capability that enables networks to automatically detect faults and reroute connections around them with minimal interruption.[28] Likewise, intrusion tolerance is an advanced technology that aims to keep critical systems functioning properly even in the face of successful intrusions.[29]

These advanced technologies underlying resilient and robust computer networks are fairly well understood, though not perfect, particularly for large-scale complex networks. Considering that DoD operates 15,000 networks involving more than seven million devices, it would be enormously challenging to implement successfully advanced technologies such as self-healing and intrusion tolerance on that scale. Implementation would require thorough changes in equipment, software, and protocols. The cost for implementation is unknown, and the required funds are not guaranteed in the budget. DoD has requested $37 billion for information technology in Fiscal Year (FY) 2013, but it encompasses a range of IT investments.[30] The budget includes $3.4 billion for cyber security efforts to protect information, information systems, and networks.

STRATEGIC INITIATIVE 2: DoD will employ new defense operating concepts to protect DoD networks and systems.

Although the strategic initiative is obviously broad and vague, the *DoD Strategy* identifies four specific actions:

1. Implement cyber hygiene best practices;

2. Address insider threats by strengthening workforce communications, workforce accountability, and internal monitoring;

3. Implement active cyber defenses against external threats; and,

4. Develop new defense operating concepts and computing architectures such as secure cloud computing.

The initiative presumes that good hygiene (e.g., updating and patching software, running antivirus software, avoiding untrusted email attachments and untrusted websites) can prevent most malicious acts. While certainly helpful, safe practices will not protect users against advanced attacks that often make use of sophisticated social engineering and zero-day exploits.

It is notoriously difficult to defend against insider threats. The strategy will depend on:

> communication, personnel training, and new technologies and processes . . . new policies, new methods of personnel training, and innovative workforce communications.[31]

The *DoD Strategy* makes a point to contrast "active" defense with traditional "passive" defense. By active defense, the *DoD Strategy* means that the network will be monitored in real time to "discover, detect, analyze, and mitigate threats and vulnerabilities,"[32] or, in other words, real-time intrusion detection and prevention. This capability aims to "stop malicious activity before it can affect DoD networks and systems."[33]

Significance and Novelty.

Generally, this strategic initiative has good ideas consistent with common sense, but the ideas are conventional and unoriginal. For example, cyber security best practices are a good idea, but best practices alone will not prevent intrusions, and the strategic initiative does not offer additional ideas beyond best practices. Also, insider threats can be ameliorated by addressing the human element in the workplace, but it is not clear how effectively the stated actions can deter insider attacks.

Perhaps the most interesting statement is emphasis on active defenses that detect and prevent intrusions in real time. This statement could be interpreted as an implicit message aimed at foreign adversaries, saying that real-time retaliation is possible. This message might help deter future attacks; the notion of deterrence is elaborated in more detail later.

Much of this strategic initiative is too broad and vague to criticize. For example, the meaning of statements like "DoD will explore new and innovative approaches and paradigms for both existing and emerging challenges"[34] is impossible to evaluate because it depends on unknowns in the future.

Practicality.

The most challenging action in this strategic initiative is active defense. Research in intrusion detection has been conducted for decades, and real-time detection is still an open question due to the continual inventiveness of resourceful adversaries. The strategic initiative does not explain how active defenses will be carried out or who will provide the technology. In general, intrusion detection can be performed by misuse detection (signature-based) or anomaly detection (behavior-based).[35] Misuse detection works for known attacks but may miss new attacks without an existing signature. On the other hand, anomaly detection may be able to detect unknown new attacks that deviate statistically from "normal" behaviors, but this approach continues to be very difficult to perfect in practice. Existing intrusion detection systems can monitor computer networks in real time, but the accuracy of detection (and hence prevention) remains uncertain.

It is not clear how new computing architectures such as cloud computing can improve DoD security. Cloud computing offers organizations benefits like lower start–up costs and capital expenditures, services on a pay–as–you–use basis, and flexibility to quickly reduce or increase capacities. However, cloud computing introduces new security risks related to data ownership, privacy, data mobility, quality of service, bandwidth, and data protection.[36]

STRATEGIC INITIATIVE 3: DoD will partner with other U.S. government departments and agencies and the private sector to enable a whole-of-government cyber security strategy.

This strategic initiative recognizes that:

> DoD's critical functions and operations rely on commercial assets, including Internet Service Providers (ISPs) and global supply chains, over which DoD has no direct authority to mitigate risk effectively.[37]

Therefore, a broad level of cooperation with other government departments and private companies is clearly necessary.

Among other government departments, the strategic initiative emphasizes DHS in particular. A notable example of cooperation was a 2010 memorandum of agreement with DHS to coordinate efforts to protect critical infrastructures and computer networks.[38] The agreement called for DoD and DHS cyber analysts to jointly support the National Cybersecurity and Communications Integration Center (NCCIC). The agreement also provides a full-time senior DHS leader and support personnel to NSA to "ensure both agencies' priorities and requests for support are clearly communicated and met."[39]

The strategic initiative also calls for public-private partnerships because the global technology supply chain affects mission critical aspects of the DoD enterprise, along with core U.S. Government and private sector functions.[40]

The partnerships will aim to "share ideas, develop new capabilities, and support collective efforts."[41] The public and private sectors will not automatically work together because of different interests. In recognition of this difficulty, the strategy describes an existing public-private partnership with the Defense Industrial Base (DIB) to increase the protection of sensitive information. DIB networks are protected under the Defense Industrial Base Cyber Security and Information Assurance program. The strategy wants additional pilot programs, business models, and policy frameworks to foster public-private synergy. Public-private partnerships will require a balance between regulation and volunteerism . . . incentives or other measures will be necessary to promote private sector participation.[42]

Significance and Novelty.

The current division of government responsibilities for protecting cyberspace is less than ideal. Broadly speaking, the DoD is responsible for defending the military networks (nominally against cyber warfare), while DHS is responsible for defending civilian government networks (against cybercrime). DHS also helps critical infrastructure owners with cyber security. At the same time, the arguably best defense capabilities reside in the DoD. It is not clear which government agency has the lead for cyber security, which would respond to a given cyber attack, and how DoD could help in the defense of civilian networks. Ideally, government agencies would work together seamlessly, but the 2009 *Cyberspace Policy Review* noted a lack of coherent policy guidance clarifying "authorities, roles, and responsibilities for cyber security-related activities across the Federal government" due to an incoherent "patchwork of Constitutional, domestic, foreign, and international laws."[43]

Public-private cooperation has been a recurrent theme in government publications on cyber security. The need for public-private partnerships was recognized in the 2003 *National Strategy to Secure Cyberspace*, which viewed public-private partnerships as useful for cyber incident response and security information sharing. It was repeated in the 2006 *National Military Strategy for Cyberspace Operations* and the DHS 2009 *National Infrastructure Protection Plan*. Considering that the private sector owns most critical infrastructures, the need for effective public-private partnerships is obvious. The question for the *DoD Strategy* is how to facilitate and incentivize cooperation. The *DoD Strategy* appears to recognize this challenge but does not offer specific plans.

Practicality.

Significant progress has been made in increasing cooperation between agencies. A few agencies—Air Force, DHS, NSA, and Federal Bureau of Investigation (FBI)—have claimed authority in cyberspace. The 24th Air Force is now the Service's component of the USCYBERCOM. As mentioned earlier, DHS and DoD have signed a memorandum of agreement. NSA is closely linked to USCYBERCOM under the same director. The FBI investigates cyber intrusions at U.S. companies but suffers from a shortage of necessary skills and support.[44]

The DHS-DoD memorandum of agreement is a good example of the *DoD Strategy's* whole-of-government approach. Whereas DoD is normally limited to defending military computer networks, the memorandum of agreement allows DoD's cyber warfare expertise to be leveraged to help DHS protect domestic networks and critical infrastructure. To fully realize the strategy's whole-of-government approach, more similar agreements will be needed that spell out how agencies can cooperate while clearly maintaining their separate missions.[45]

The *DoD Strategy* is vague about specific means of public-private cooperation, but an obvious example is information sharing about vulnerabilities and threats. The *DoD Strategy* points out an example of the DIB pilot. It involves DoD, DHS, and 20 companies, including ISPs and defense contractors. Threat signature information is shared by USCYBERCOM and NSA with the participating companies. In addition, there are various pending legislations to increase information sharing between private companies and the government.

An amended version of the Cyber Intelligence Sharing and Protection Act (CISPA) bill passed the House of Representatives in April 2012. It contains provisions for private companies to "use cyber security systems to identify and obtain cyber threat information," share this information with the government, and be protected from lawsuits for these actions.[46] Civil liberty groups have expressed concerns that vague wording in the bill might allow companies to collect unlimited private information about Internet users under the pretext of suspicious activities.

The Strengthening and Enhancing Cybersecurity by Using Research, Education, Information, and Technology Act of 2012 (the SECURE IT Act) was introduced into the Senate in March 2012. Similar to CISPA, the SECURE IT Act is aimed at facilitating information sharing in regard to cyber threats. The SECURE IT Act has likewise been criticized for insufficient protection of existing privacy rights.

A revised version of the Cybersecurity Act of 2012 (CSA) failed to pass the Senate in August 2012. Title I called for a public-private consortium to develop a set of voluntary cyber security practices for protecting critical national infrastructure. However, existing governmental regulators with authority over any critical national infrastructure could require regulated companies to comply with the "voluntary" cyber security practices. Businesses have expressed concerns about the potential costs for compliance. Title VII was similar in intention to the CISPA and SECURE IT Act bills to encourage network monitoring and information sharing by private companies, with legal protection provided to companies. Cyber threat information could be shared with law enforcement through civilian "cyber security exchanges" only where the information pertains to a cybercrime, imminent threat of bodily harm or serious injury, or serious threat to minors. DHS would develop privacy policies for how shared information would be used by the government. After the failure of CSA to pass the Senate, some senators pressured the White House to issue an executive order for voluntary cyber security guidelines for owners of power, water, and other critical infrastructure facilities.

Public-private cooperation is not easy due to conflicting interests. The GAO has noted efforts to develop new information sharing arrangements between the private sector and the government.[47] However, "expectations of private sector stakeholders are not being met by their federal partners in areas related to sharing information about cyber-based threats."[48] Historically, industry has tended to resist new regulations for reasons of cost. In regard to cyber security practices, companies have argued that they know their networks better and can adapt faster to new threats than government regulators. Consequently, the government is currently focused on voluntary actions, but it recognizes that incentives will be necessary. For companies, information sharing is a complicated economic question with advantages balanced by drawbacks.[49]

STRATEGIC INITIATIVE 4: DoD will build robust relationships with U.S. allies and international partners to strengthen collective cyber security.

This strategic initiative is aimed primarily at other nations to foster cooperation for "collective self-defense and collective deterrence" through timely sharing of information about "cyber events, threat signatures of malicious code, and information about emerging actors and threats."[50] Other shared activities include capacity building, training, dialogue about best practices, and pursuit of "international cyberspace norms and principles that promote openness, interoperability, security, and reliability."[51]

Significance and Novelty.

This strategic initiative emphasizes the advantages of collective self-defense to appeal not only to close allies but also to "a wider pool of allied and partner militaries" and "like-minded states."[52] The advantages of international cooperation for cyber security are obvious, and the notion has been repeated in government publications leading back to at least the 2003 *National Strategy to Secure Cyberspace*. The notion of collective self-defense in warfare (not just in cyberspace) goes even further back to the North Atlantic Treaty Organization (NATO) established in 1949.

Interestingly, the Article 5 "mutual defense" clause of NATO has already been tested by cyber attacks. In April 2007, the Estonian government had decided to move the Bronze Soldier of Tallinn, triggering Russian protests. Multiple waves of distributed denial of service (DDoS) attacks hit the websites of the Estonian parliament, banks, ministries, newspapers,and media. The Estonian Foreign Minister promptly accused the Kremlin of responsibility, raising the question of whether NATO member countries would respond collectively to the DDoS attacks. Experts sent to Estonia concluded that the DDoS attacks were not sufficiently serious for Article 5 but highlighted the need for clear legal definitions on cyber attacks that would qualify for Article 5 mutual defense.

It is not clear that the NATO model of collective self-defense, reflecting a simplistic "us versus them" mindset reminiscent of the Cold War, is appropriate for a more complicated modern world. Today, major nations cooperate on many levels while still competing in cyberspace. For example, China is heavily invested in U.S. assets, and the Chinese economy depends critically on trade with the United States. However, at the same time, China is reportedly fully engaged in cyber espionage activities.[53]

In addition to collective self-defense, the strategic initiative states that international cooperation raises the question of deterrence. By conventional wisdom, strength in numbers could be an effective deterrent to future cyber attacks. The notion of deterrence has not been a major theme in previous government publications, except the *2010 Comprehensive National Cybersecurity Initiative* mentioned deterrence as part of one of its major goals. However, it is questionable whether deterrence is possible in cyber warfare in the same way that nuclear deterrence worked by fear of "mutually assured destruction."[54]

Practicality.

This strategic initiative raises two questions of practicality: can the United States forge treaties for effective international cooperation, and can collective deterrence work in cyber security? New international treaties to cooperate in cyberspace would have to overcome considerable obstacles: (1) competing interests, (2) different attitudes toward cyber warfare, (3) different definitions of malicious cyber acts (e.g., starting with "cyber warfare"), and (4) difficult enforceability (e.g., of terms limiting proliferation of cyber weapons).

The Council of Europe Convention on Cyber-crime might give hope for international cooperation on cyber warfare. Ratified in July 2004, it is the only binding international treaty on cybercrime.[55] Though it remains mostly limited to Europe, it is open to non-European states and has been signed by the United States. It provides guidelines for all governments wishing to develop legislation against cybercrime. It also provides a framework for international cooperation. However, while all nations have an interest in controlling cybercrime, different nations have competing interests in cyber warfare.

In 1998, Russia proposed a treaty banning cyber attacks for military purposes, but the United States has been reluctant to consider any limitations on its freedom to act in cyberspace. In July 2010, the United States shifted its position to join a group of other nations, including China and Russia, on United Nations (UN) recommendations to create norms of accepted behavior in cyberspace, exchange information on national cyber security strategies, and strengthen cyber security in less developed countries.

In September 2011, Russia and several allies, including China, proposed the International Code of Conduct for Information Security to the UN to standardize a code of responsible behavior in cyberspace. The United States opposed the proposal on the grounds that it sought to shift governance of the Internet (which is currently done by various U.S.-based nongovernmental international organizations) to authoritarian regimes that might attempt to curb the open culture of the Internet. Russia is continuing efforts for a global treaty on cyber security but, so far, the proposals appear unlikely to be successful due to opposition from Western countries. There is no reason for the United States to enter agreements that hinder its freedom to act in cyberspace.

Whereas a global treaty on behaviour norms appears to be unlikely, strategic treaties with allies and "like-minded states" are more feasible and advantageous, following a NATO model, for instance. Benefits, including shared threat intelligence and early attack warning, are easy to imagine. On the other hand, the *DoD Strategy* mentions the benefit of "collective deterrence," which is more questionable. Presumably, it refers to the notion that adversaries would refrain from attacking due to the "strength in numbers" of a U.S. alliance. Following the logic of nuclear deterrence, an adversary should believe that a U.S. alliance possesses the capability for retaliation and destruction on a scale that the adversary cannot accept.[56]

Unfortunately, the cyber environment is completely different from the nuclear environment, where nuclear weapons can be traced and counted. In order to be effective, cyber deterrence must overcome a few practical obstacles.[57] The first and most obvious problem is attribution—identification of the real source of a cyber attack. Cyber attacks can be anonymized in many ways (e.g., by using proxies or stolen computer accounts). The Internet is not well equipped to traceback packets and, in the best case, might identify an Internet protocol (IP) address. For malware attacks, the creator is very difficult to discover from code disassembly.

The second practical problem, if attribution can be solved, is credible capacity for destructive retaliation. Few doubt the offensive capability of the United States, but it has not been demonstrated yet. In cyber warfare, there is no real reason to reveal "cyber weapons" unnecessarily. There is concern that revelations of U.S. full offensive capability could trigger a global cyber arms race. Also, a software cyber weapon could be reverse engineered by an unfriendly country.

A third problem is demonstrated willingness to retaliate with destructive force. The United States has not issued specific conditions for retaliation but has left all options open. The *2011 International Strategy for Cyberspace* declared:

> When warranted, the United States will respond to hostile acts in cyberspace as we would to any other threat to our country.[58]

Furthermore, the United States will reserve the right to use all necessary means—diplomatic, informational, military, and economic—as appropriate and consistent with applicable international law, in order to defend our Nation, our allies, our partners, and our interests.[59]

STRATEGIC INITIATIVE 5: DoD will leverage the nation's ingenuity through an exceptional cyber workforce and rapid technological innovation.

This strategic initiative aims to maintain U.S. superiority through investment in its people, technology, and R&D to create and sustain the cyberspace capabilities.[60]

The first part of the strategy consists of improvements made to personnel recruiting and hiring. Specific ideas include:
- Streamlining hiring practices;
- Exchange programs to allow for "no penalty" cross-flow of cyber professionals between the public and private sectors;

- Cross-generational mentoring programs;
- Development of Reserve and National Guard cyber capabilities; and,
- Exchanges and continuing education programs.

The second part of the strategy addresses investment in technology, rather than people, by revising processes for acquisition of information technology. The new process will adopt five principles:

1. Reducing DoD's acquisition processes and regulations to cycles of 12 to 36 months;

2. Incremental development and testing instead of a single deployment of large, complex systems;

3. Sacrificing some customization to speed up incremental improvements;

4. Adopting differing levels of oversight based on DoD's prioritization of critical systems; and,

5. Improving security measures for all purchased software and hardware, using an in-depth security approach.

The strategic initiative points to the National Cyber Range as a means to "test and evaluate new cyberspace concepts, policies, and technologies."[61] In addition, companies will be incentivized through "initiatives such as Small Business Innovation Research, creative joint ventures, and targeted investments."[62]

Significance and Novelty.

For the most part, this strategic initiative does not say much new. The need for a well-trained workforce is an obvious theme repeated in previous government publications. Hopefully, DoD has already started to build up its cyber workforce. The need for technology innovation is also obvious, considering the rapid rate of progress in information technologies. The last point about incentivizing companies somewhat repeats Strategic Initiative 3.

It might be argued that this strategic initiative is already ongoing. Its general purpose is not to propose revolutionary actions but to declare a message to mainly two audiences: the private sector and foreign adversaries. To the private sector, the strategy conveys an intention to acquire new defense technologies and hire cyber professionals. To foreign adversaries, the message is DoD's intention to achieve and maintain superiority in cyberspace.

The strategy is incomplete in addressing R&D. While the strategic initiative aims for "technological innovation," it gives much more attention to the DoD acquisition process than to investment in R&D. It is not clear how innovations will be stimulated. For example, nothing is mentioned about investment in universities or scientific labs for basic research, or how basic research will be translated into new products to acquire. It seems to be implicitly assumed that small businesses will automatically innovate.

Practicality.

The actions in this strategic initiative are straightforward and hopefully already on their way to implementation. Unfortunately, this strategic initiative appears to depend highly on defense funding.

An agile acquisition process is being implemented by the Defense Advanced Research Projects Agency (DARPA). An example is the Cyber Fast Track program that strives to fund small research projects with rapid approval (perhaps less than a week).[63] The research projects are carried out by individuals or small groups for a few months. Hopefully, the short timescales will lead to better adaptiveness to quickly changing security threats.

CRITICAL OBSERVATIONS

After reading and evaluating each strategic initiative, some general observations about the unclassified version of the *DoD Strategy for Operating in Cyberspace* can be made.

- The strategy focuses mostly on technology, resources, and cooperation. Human resources are addressed only in part of the last initiative.
- The strategy emphasizes defense and prevention. The classified version of the strategy obviously includes more points (e.g., presumably offensive capabilities).
- The strategic initiatives mostly repeat themes that have appeared in previous government publications. The ideas are uncontroversial and sensible, but no surprising ideas are really offered.

- Some of the actions are already in progress, such as treating cyberspace as an operational domain; active defense; public-private cooperation; cyber workforce recruiting; and rapid technology acquisition. In this sense, the *DoD Strategy* is mostly an affirmation of current directions.
- The strategy does not offer solutions to several practical challenges, such as how to implement advanced technologies for network resilience and robustness into DoD's computer networks; how to accurately detect intrusions in real time; how to properly incentivize private sector information sharing; and how to effectively deter cyber attacks.
- The strategy does not distinguish between different types of adversaries—nation-states, foreign intelligence, hacktivists, criminals, hackers, terrorists—nor does the strategy address initiatives for specific types of adversaries.
- The unclassified version of the strategy neglects to address important issues: offense; attribution; rules for proper response to cyber attacks; and metrics of progress toward implementation. These issues are discussed here.

Offense.

The unclassified *DoD Strategy for Operating in Cyberspace* is primarily concerned with defensive protection of the information infrastructure. However, it is obvious that the United States, like all modern nations, would be foolish not to build up offensive as well as defensive capabilities. The 2004 *National Military Strategy of the United States of America* stated plainly that cyber capabilities, "both offensive and defensive, are key to ensuring U.S. freedom of action across the battlespace."[64] Also, the Air Force has said "cyberspace operations seek to ensure freedom of action across all domains for U.S. forces and allies, and deny that same freedom to adversaries," implying the capability for offense.[65]

It has been reported that the United States and Israel were responsible for developing the Stuxnet malware aimed at sabotaging the Natanz uranium enrichment plant in Iran.[66] Stuxnet spread through the internal computer network in search of programmable logic controllers controlling gas centrifuges and reportedly spun the centrifuges at rates outside of their normal operating range, causing perhaps a thousand centrifuges to fail. If true, Stuxnet would qualify as the first "cyber weapon" launched by one nation to damage another's physical infrastructure. Shortly after Stuxnet was discovered, it was suspected of belonging to a growing arsenal of U.S. cyber weapons.[67]

A strategy for building offensive capability has not been stated, most likely because of concern about stimulating a global cyber arms race. If an offensive strategy will be developed, it should include clear guidelines for how and when offensive actions can be carried out against another nation.

Attribution.

The *DoD Strategy* does not specifically address the problem of attribution. As mentioned earlier, attribution is an enormous challenge, and the plausible deniability afforded by anonymity is a great contributing factor to cyber attacks. Adversaries are encouraged by the fact that the real source of attacks can be easily hidden. Even if an adversary is suspected, there is typically no hard evidence proving the perpetrator of an attack.

Technically, the real source is easy to hide because the Internet was not designed to validate source IP addresses, traceback packets, or record details of packets along their routes (due to the vast volumes of traffic). Even if packets could be traced back to an IP address, adversaries could confuse trace back by using anonymizing proxies or hijacked accounts as intermediaries. Moreover, many attacks are carried out by malware, and the creator of malware is very difficult to discover from disassembling the malware code. In addition, the lack of international laws hinders traceback when packets cross national boundaries.

Rules for Proper Response to Cyber Attacks.

Given capabilities for offense and attribution, retaliation for cyber attacks is possible. Retaliation might consist of a physical response, which is implied by the declaration of cyberspace to be an operational domain, risking the possibility of a cyber attack escalating into a conventional war. However, the unclassified *DoD Strategy for Operating in Cyberspace* is silent on guidelines for proper response, i.e., what is the threshold for military response, and what qualifies as "use of force"? Guidelines must take into account the difficulty of attribution and assessment of damages in the cyber domain.

It has been reported that President Obama signed executive orders in June 2011 describing rules of engagement for U.S. military commanders in carrying out cyber attacks and other computer-based operations against other countries. The orders supposedly provide guidance on when presidential approval is needed to initiate attacks and on conditions when the military can respond to an intrusion by active retaliation.

A strategy should address two issues. First, when does a cyber attack justify a military response? DoD reportedly has been considering an idea of "equivalence." For example, a conventional response could be warranted if a cyber attack results in the same level of death or physical damage that a conventional military attack would cause. A traditional legal test is the "Caroline Test," where potential forcible actions taken by states for self-defense may be considered to be lawful only if they are subject to the three conditions of immediacy, necessity, and proportionality.[68] The first two conditions mean that the threat is imminent, and peaceful alternatives are not an option. These conditions would probably be easy to meet in the event of a major cyber attack. The third condition means that the response should be proportional to the threat. This condition may be the most challenging to meet due to the interconnected nature of computer networks.

Michael Schmitt has proposed a more elaborate framework, considering the intensity of damage in each of seven areas (severity, immediacy, directness, invasiveness, measurability, presumptive legitimacy, and responsibility) to assess the composite effects of a cyber attack.[69]

The second question that should be addressed is, What is an appropriate response? Traditional wars are guided by the Laws of Armed Conflict (LOAC) derived from a series of international treaties, such as the Geneva conventions, as well as traditional practices that the United States and other nations consider customary international law. Obviously cyber warfare is not covered by existing treaties, but the question is whether the principles of LOAC—military necessity, distinction, and proportionality—should be applicable to cyber warfare. Military necessity refers to restrictions on combat actions to only those necessary to accomplish a legitimate military objective. Distinction refers to restriction of combat targets to valid military targets (versus noncombatant targets such as civilians, civilian property, and prisoners of war). Proportionality is a restriction on excessive use of force beyond that needed to accomplish the military objective.

Metrics of Progress.

For a long time, the field of security has lacked a mathematical science to answer two fundamentally important questions: How far has the DoD Strategy been implemented, and how secure are U.S. assets? Today, it is difficult to quantify the security of a computer system.[70] Therefore, it is hard to have confidence or trust in a protected system. In current practice, security is assessed experimentally by the number of vulnerabilities found or the results of penetration testing (or red teaming).

The closest thing to science in security may be risk management. The mathematics behind risk management may give the appearance of precision, but input parameters such as likelihood of attacks are notoriously difficult to estimate. As a result, the calculations of risk are essentially best guesses. There is no way to verify calculated risks; even the precision of calculated risks is hard to quantify.

The *DoD Strategy* does not address the need for cyber security metrics that are currently missing. It may be possible to measure actions taken in each of the strategic initiatives, but in the end, little could be proven about the strength of cyber security of U.S. assets without appropriate metrics.

CONCLUSIONS AND RECOMMENDATIONS

DoD faces a rapidly changing environment of cyber threats. Fortunately, DoD is one of the best prepared organizations in the world. As noted earlier, it has undertaken many actions to fortify its capabilities (such as establishment of the USCYBERCOM) and defensive position to protect the nation's military networks and critical infrastructures.

With the *DoD Strategy for Operating in Cyberspace*, important messages have been conveyed to the American public, other government agencies, the private sector, and other nations. The most important message is that the DoD is serious about taking further actions to maintain superiority in cyberspace. Another message is recognition that neither the DoD (nor any single agency) can protect all of cyberspace by itself, and the DoD is appealing for cooperation from the private sector and like-minded nations.

The ultimate question is whether the strategy is adequate to maintain DoD superiority in the face of existing and future cyber threats. The GAO describes a complete national cyber strategy as one that:
- Includes well-defined strategic objectives;
- Provides understandable goals for the government and the private sector;
- Articulates cyber priorities among the objectives;
- Provides a futuristic vision of what secure cyberspace should be;

- Seeks to integrate federal government capabilities;
- Establishes metrics to gauge progress against the strategy; and,
- Provides enforcement and accountability in the event of progress shortfalls.[71]

The *DoD Strategy for Operating in Cyberspace* falls short in this list. For example, it is not clear about priorities, futuristic vision, progress metrics, or enforcement and accountability. Some of these inadequacies were already mentioned in an earlier section. It is important to recognize that the *DoD Strategy* will undoubtedly be revised; strategies must continually evolve to adapt to the changing threat landscape. After reading and evaluating each strategic initiative in the current *DoD Strategy*, recommendations for future versions of the strategy include:

- Expansion of detailed plans of actions to take for each strategic initiative;
- Explanations of how to find solutions to practical challenges (e.g., how to implement advanced technologies for network resilience and robustness on a large scale, how to accurately detect and prevent intrusions in real time, how to determine effective incentives for private sector information sharing);
- Elaboration on specific strategies to address different types of adversaries who have different capabilities, skills, and goals;
- Elaboration on specific mechanisms to stimulate technological innovations and translate research results into new defense products;
- Additional consideration of omitted issues, including attribution, rules for proper response to cyber attacks, and security metrics; and

- Proposals of novel, forward-looking ideas and new ways of thinking (e.g., effective cyber deterrence).

It should be straightforward for future versions of the *DoD Strategy* to fill in the recommended details. Perhaps a greater concern is a noticeable lack of novel ideas. The *DoD Strategy* mostly deals with activities already in progress, which are probably not much different from ongoing activities in other nations. The *DoD Strategy* neglects to identify unique U.S. advantages and resources, and how to capitalize on these unique traits to maintain U.S. superiority. In the absence of a unique strategy, the United States may very well be able to build effective defensive and offensive capabilities, but it faces the risk of losing a superior advantage if other nations reach parity by doing the same things.

ENDNOTES

1. Robert M. Gates, "Submitted Statement to Senate Armed Services Committee," Hearing before Senate Armed Services Committee, U.S. Senate, January 27, 2009, p. 8.

2. James Adams, "Testimony of James Adams, Chief Executive Officer Infrastructure Defense, Inc.," Hearing before Committee on Governmental Affairs, U.S. Senate, March 2, 2000.

3. Nathan Thornburgh, "The Invasion of the Chinese Cyberspies," August 29, 2005, available from *www.time.com/time/magazine/article/0,9171,1098961-1,00.html*.

4. U.S.-China Economic and Security Review Commission, "2009 Report to Congress of the U.S.-China Economic and Security Review Commission," Washington, DC: U.S. Government Printing Office, November 2009, pp. 167-180.

5. William J. Lynn, III, "Remarks on the Department of Defense Cyber Strategy," Speech at the National Defense University, Washington, DC, July 14, 2011.

6. "The National Strategy to Secure Cyberspace," Washington, DC: The White House, February 2003, *available from www.us-cert.gov/reading_room/cyberspace_strategy.pdf.*

7. Chairman of the Joint Chiefs of Staff, "The National Military Strategy of the United States of America," Washington, DC: Joint Chiefs of Staff, 2004, available from *www.defense.gov/news/mar2005/d20050318nms.pdf.*

8. Chairman of the Joint Chiefs of Staff, "The National Military Strategy for Cyberspace Operations," Washington, DC: Joint Chiefs of Staff, December 2006, available from *www.dod.mil/pubs/foi/joint_staff/jointStaff_jointOperations/07-F-2105doc1.pdf.*

9. *Securing Cyberspace for the 44th Presidency, A Report of the CSIS Commission on Cybersecurity for the 44th Presidency,* Washington, DC: Center for Strategic and International Studies, December 2008.

10. "The Comprehensive National Cybersecurity Initiative (CNCI)," Washington, DC: The White House, March 2, 2010, available from *www.whitehouse.gov/sites/default/files/cybersecurity.pdf.*

11. David Powner, "National Cybersecurity Strategy: Key Improvements are Needed to Strengthen the Nation's Posture," GAO-09-432T, Washington, DC: Government Accountability Office, March 10, 2009.

12. "National Infrastructure Protection Plan: Partnering to Enhance Protection and Resiliency," Washington, DC: U.S. Department of Homeland Security, 2009, available from *www.dhs.gov/xlibrary/assets/NIPP_Plan.pdf.*

13. "International Strategy for Cyberspace: Prosperity, Security, and Openness in a Networked World," Washington, DC: The White House, May 2011, available from *www.whitehouse.gov/sites/default/files/rss_viewer/internationalstrategy_cyberspace.pdf.*

14. *Ibid.*

15. "Department of Defense Strategy for Operating in Cyberspace," Washington, DC: Department of Defense, July 2011, available from *www.defense.gov/news/d20110714cyber.pdf.*

16. William J. Lynn III, "Defending a New Domain: The Pentagon's Cyberstrategy," Washington, DC: U.S. Department of Defense, available from *www.defense.gov/home/features/2010/0410_cybersec/lynn-article1.aspx.*

17. "DoD Announces First Strategy for Operating in Cyberspace," Washington, DC: Department of Defense, July, 14, 2001, available from *www.defense.gov/releases/release.aspx? releaseid=14651.*

18. "Department of Defense Strategy for Operating in Cyberspace," p. 5.

19. "Cyber Storm: Securing Cyber Space," Washington, DC: Department of Homeland Security, available from *www.dhs.gov/cyber-storm-securing-cyber-space.*

20. "The National Military Strategy of the United States of America."

21. Michael W. Wynne, "Cyberspace as a domain in which the Air Force flies and fights," Speech at the C41SR Integration Conference, Crystal City, VA, November 2, 2006.

22. Siobhan Gorman and Julian Barnes, "Cyber Combat: Act of War," May 30, 2011, available from *online.wsj.com/article/SB100 01424052702304563104576355623135782718.html.*

23. "Pentagon Unveils New Offensive Cybersecurity Strategy," Washington, DC: RFE/RL, July 15, 2011, available from *www.rferl.org/content/pentagon_unveils_new_offensive_cybersecurity_strategy/24266548.html.*

24. Davi D'Agostino and Greg Wilshusen, "Defense Department Cyber Efforts: DoD Faces Challenges in Its Cyber Activities," GAO-11-75, Washington, DC: Government Accountability Office, July 2011.

25. *Ibid.*

26. Davi D'Agostino, "Defense Department Cyber Efforts: More Detailed Guidance Needed to Ensure Military Services Develop Appropriate Cyberspace Capabilities," GAO-11-421, Washington, DC: Government Accountability Office, May 2011.

27. David Clark, "The Design Philosophy of the DARPA Internet Protocols," *Computer Communication Review*, Vol. 18, No. 4, August 1988, pp. 106–114.

28. C. Green, "Protocols for a Self-Healing Network," paper presented at IEEE Military Communications Conference (MILCOM '95), November 6, 1995, pp. 252-256.

29. Yves Deswarte and David Powell, "Internet Security: an Intrusion-Tolerance Approach," Proceedings of the IEEE, Vol. 94, No. 2, February 2006, pp. 432-441.

30. Cheryl Pellerin, "DoD Develops Cyberspace Rules of Engagement," March 23, 2012, available from *science.dodlive. mil/2012/03/23/dod-develops-cyberspace-rules-of-engagement/*.

31. "Department of Defense Strategy for Operating in Cyberspace," p. 7.

32. *Ibid.*

33. *Ibid.*

34. *Ibid.*

35. Ryan Trost, *Practical Intrusion Analysis: Prevention and Detection for the Twenty-First Century*, Upper Saddle River, NJ: Addison Wesley, 2009.

36. Ronald Krutz and Russell Vines, *Cloud Security: a Comprehensive Guide to Secure Cloud Computing*, New York: John Wiley and Sons, 2010.

37. "Department of Defense Strategy for Operating in Cyberspace," p. 8.

38. "Memorandum of Agreement Between the Department of Homeland Security and the Department of Justice Regarding Cybersecurity," Washington, DC: Department of Homeland Security, available from *www.dhs.gov/xlibrary/assets/20101013-dod-dhs-cyber-moa.pdf*.

39. *Ibid.*

40. "Department of Defense Strategy for Operating in Cyberspace," p. 9.

41. *Ibid.*

42. *Ibid.*

43. Peter Fox, "Domestic Cybersecurity Requires Clearer Federal Roles and Responsibilities," March 2012, available from *www.americanbar.org/content/dam/aba/publications/law_practice_today/domestic-cyber-security-requires-clearer-federal-roles-and-responsibilities.authcheckdam.pdf*.

44. Office of the Inspector General Audit Division, "Federal Bureau of Investigation's Ability to Address the National Security Cyber Intrusion Threat," Washington, DC: U.S. Department of Justice, April 2011, available from *www.justice.gov/oig/reports/FBI/a1122r.pdf*.

45. Fox.

46. H.R. 3523 "Cyber Intelligence Sharing and Protection Act," Washington, DC: U.S. Government Printing office, available from *www.gpo.gov/fdsys/pkg/BILLS-112hr3523rfs/pdf/BILLS-112hr3523rfs.pdf*.

47. David A. Powner, "Critical Infrastructure Protection: Key Private and Public Cyber Expectations Need to Be Consistently Addressed," GAO-10-628, Washington, DC: Government Accountability Office, July 2010.

48. Gregory C. Wilshusen, "Cybersecurity: Continued Attention Needed to Protect Our Nation's Critical Infrastructure," GAO-11-865T, Washington, DC: Government Accountability Office, July 2011.

49. Esther Gal-Or and Anindya Ghose, "The Economic Incentives for Sharing Security Information," *Information Systems Research*, Vol. 16, No. 2, June 2005, pp. 186–208.

50. "Department of Defense Strategy for Operating in Cyberspace," p. 9.

51. "Department of Defense Strategy for Operating in Cyberspace," p. 10.

52. *Ibid.*

53. "Occupying the Information High Ground: Chinese Capabilities for Computer Network Operations and Cyber Espionage, U.S.-China Economic and Security Review Commission," Baltimore, MD: Northrop Grumman Corp, March 7, 2012.

54. Eric Sterner, "Retaliatory Deterrence in Cyberspace," *Strategic Studies Quarterly*, Spring 2011, pp. 62-80.

55. "Convention on Cybercrime," The Hague, The Netherlands: Council of Europe, available from *conventions.coe.int/Treaty/en/Treaties/Html/185.htm*.

56. Matthew Crosston, "World Gone Cyber MAD," *Strategic Studies Quarterly*, Spring 2011, pp. 100-116.

57. David Elliott, "Deterring Strategic Cyberattack," *IEEE Security and Privacy*, Vol. 9, No. 5, September/October 2011, pp. 36-40.

58. "International Strategy for Cyberspace: Prosperity, Security, and Openness in a Networked World."

59. *Ibid.*

60. "Department of Defense Strategy for Operating in Cyberspace," p. 10.

61. "Department of Defense Strategy for Operating in Cyberspace," p. 12.

62. *Ibid.*

63. Dawn Lim, "DARPA's New Fast Track Okays Hacker Projects in Just Seven Days," November 14, 2011, available from *www.wired.com/dangerroom/2011/11/darpa-fast-track/*.

64. "The National Military Strategy of the United States of America."

65. "Cyberspace Operations Air Force Doctrine Document 3-12," Washington, DC: U.S. Air Force, November 2011, available from *www.docstoc.com/docs/137067830/AF-Cyberspace-Operations-Doctrine-AFDD3-12.*

66. David Sanger, "Obama Order Sped Up Wave of Cyber-attacks Against Iran," June 1, 2012, available from *www.nytimes.com/2012/06/01/world/middleeast/obama-ordered-wave-of-cyberat-tacks-against-iran.html.*

67. Ellen Nakashima, "U.S. Accelerating Cyberweapon Research," March 19, 2012, available from *www.washington-post.com/world/national-security/us-accelerating-cyberweapon-re-search/2012/03/13/gIQAMRGVLS_story.html.*

68. Dimitrios Delibasis, "State Use of Force in Cyberspace for Self-Defence: A New Challenge for a New Century," *Peace Conflict and Development: An Interdisciplinary Journal*, Issue 8, February 2006, available from *www.academia.edu/1796665/State_Use_of_Force_in_Cyberspace_for_Self-Defence_A_New_Challenge_for_a_New_Century.*

69. James B. Michel et al., "Measured Responses to Cyber At-tacks Using Schmitt Analysis: a Case Study of Attack Scenarios for a Software-Intensive System," paper presented at 27th Annual International Software and Applications Conf., Dallas, TX, No-vember 3-6, 2003, pp. 622-626.

70. Sal Stolfo et al., "Measuring Security," *IEEE Security and Privacy*, Vol. 9, No. 3, May/June 2011, pp. 60-65.

71. Powner, "National Cybersecurity Strategy: Key Improvements Are Needed to Strengthen the Nation's Posture," pp. 7-8.

www.ingramcontent.com/pod-product-compliance
Lightning Source LLC
Chambersburg PA
CBHW080624290526
45790CB00007B/2912